School
Smarts

Nancy Golden

Children's Press®
A Division of Scholastic Inc.
New York / Toronto / London / Auckland / Sydney
Mexico City / New Delhi / Hong Kong
Danbury, Connecticut

Thanks to the Westown School, Westown, PA.

Book Design: Michael DeLisio
Contributing Editor: Matthew Pitt
Photo Credits: All photos by Maura B. McConnell

Library of Congress Catalaoging-in-Publication Data

Golden, Nancy (Nancy L.)
School smarts / by Nancy Golden.
    p. cm. -- (Smarts)
Includes index.
Summary: Provides tips for teens on time management, study skills,
finding help when it is needed, and test-taking skills to get the most
out of one's school years and to prepare for life after high school or
college.
ISBN 0-516-23930-9 (lib. bdg.) -- ISBN 0-516-24015-3 (pbk.)
1. Study skills--Juvenile literature. [1. Study skills. 2. Test-taking
skills. 3. Time management.] I. Title. II. Series.
LB1049 .G65 2002
371.3'028'1--dc21

                              2002002072

Contents

It's hard to keep your mind from wandering when you feel like you have to be in two places at once.

It hits you on Monday morning, all at once.

Your friends ask when you'll have time to hang out. You think about your busy week and your packed schedule. It feels like a slap in the face. You have one test on Wednesday and two on Thursday. That's not all. You have a science project due Friday, a bunch of household chores, and four days of basketball practice! How will you do it all? And how will you do it well?

Let's face it. Juggling so many things at once can be difficult. But knowing how to organize your time is a skill you can use forever. Once you learn the skill, you'll be able to keep your schoolwork—and your life—moving smoothly. With a little planning, you can do it! This book will teach you how to use study skills to budget your time wisely. It will also reveal a few test-taking techniques. With just a little extra effort, you'll be making the most of your school years.

Each teacher runs his or her class in a different way. To be a successful student, you need to know what is expected of you in each class.

Chapter 1

You Aren't Alone

Things seemed so much simpler when you were in elementary school. You had less work and responsibility. You've come a long way since then. You have more schoolwork. You have more responsibilities. Yet you have less time to get everything done. You have to find ways to use your time efficiently. One way is to seek out people who can help you.

Teachers

Your teachers are your most direct link to learning. It's important to find out what each teacher's expectations are. This may help you understand how they determine your grade. Teachers can let you know the penalties for missed homework, or

how you can earn extra credit. They should also tell you when they will be available to offer some extra guidance to students. Some teachers offer extra help every week. Others provide extra help just before tests.

These work sessions can make a difference. You get more individual attention, and show your teacher that you're serious about succeeding.

Guidance Counselors

Guidance counselors have different responsibilities, depending on the school. Some help solve problems with your schedule. Others give advice to students who are struggling with a certain class. All guidance counselors are available for the students. Be sure to find out their office hours and check in with them from time to time.

Peer Tutors

In-school tutors help students with class work before or after school. The tutors may be your age, older students, or even recent graduates. These kids

Experienced school guidance counselors have seen it all. If you're having troubles, they can help you see your way through even the toughest of problems.

have been through it before, so they can give you valuable tips.

Managing Your Time

Sometimes there don't seem to be enough hours in the day to complete your work. The good news is that with a little planning, you can make your life a whole lot easier.

Examining Your Week

The first thing to do is to look at the commitments you already have. Usually, certain days of the week are busier or quieter for us. By knowing which days are which, you can create a smarter work schedule for yourself.

Using a calendar or a student organizer, plot out a typical week. First, fill in all your regular weekly activities—such as sports practice, homework, or after-school jobs. Once you've done that, you'll have a good sense of which days are packed and which leave you with a little free time.

Jotting down your duties and commitments onto a calendar is a great idea. It will help give you a sense of how much (or how little!) spare time you have.

Breaking It Down

Your typical schedule will provide clues on how to approach major tasks—from science projects to final exams!

Do you have a project due in two weeks? Instead of thinking of it as a whole project, think of it as a series of mini-assignments. Don't forget to

My Project Calendar

SUNDAY	MONDAY	TUESDAY	WEDNESDAY	THURSDAY	FRIDAY	SATURDAY
3 Social Studies (SS): get books for project (due on 22nd!) from library	**4** review (rev.) how to divide fractions for Friday's test Band Practice	**5** rev. how to multiply fractions for Friday's test B-ball practice	**6** rev. adding & subtract fractions! SS: take notes from book 1 Math x-tra help	**7** take sample test fractions! SS: collect Web sites for project B-ball practice	**8** (Math test – fractions!) Baby-sit for Kemps	**9** SS: take notes from book 2 B-ball game Party at Jesse's
10 SS: take notes from book 3 Grandma's birthday party	**11** SS: take notes from Web sites; look for pictures Band Practice	**12** SS: Write plansheet for report B-ball practice	**13** SS: Begin draft for report Science (Sci): rev. chapter (ch.) 2 pgs. 35–43 Science x-tra help Dentist 5:00	**14** SS: continue work on draft Sci: rev. ch. 2 pgs. 43–48 B-ball practice	**15** Sci: rev. ch. 3 pgs. 51–57	**16** SS: Put together pix and graph Sci: rev. ch. 2 pgs. 57–60 B-ball practice
17 SS: Begin final copy Sci: make up sample test	**18** Science x-tra help Band Practice	**19** (Science test – ch. 2& 3) SS: Finish final copy B-ball practice	**20** SS: Put project together. Have Mom proofread. Dentist 4:00	**21** SS: Final check of project B-ball practice	**22** (SS Project DUE TODAY!)	**23** B-ball game A.M.
24	**25**	**26**	**27**	**28**	**29**	**30**

Spring Break!

write down the final due date the moment your teacher assigns the project.

Break down your project into steps. Maybe one part focuses on library research, and another part deals with drawing illustrations. A third step may involve reading from chapters in your textbook. Don't let all these parts overwhelm you. Decide how much time you might need for each part. Create a due date for each part of the project. Plot it out on your calendar.

On days where you have a lot of commitments, give yourself less to do. On days where you have fewer commitments, try working more on the project. An organized schedule is easier to work with than trying to juggle all your tasks in your head.

Here's a good idea: Make your final due date two days before it's due to the teacher. That will give you extra time if you need it. Do the same thing for any scheduled tests you have. Plan to have your studying done ahead of the test date. Then, you can use the last couple of days for reviewing your notes.

By breaking your big project down into smaller steps, you'll help make your workload more manageable.

Having a heap of homework at night can bring you down. Yet a comforting and inviting study area can lighten your mood.

Chapter 2

Bring It on Home

It's important to bring home the right books and notes each night. Yet sometimes you can forget to bring home a few things, especially if you've had a hectic school day. Here's something to try when the bell rings after each class: Jot down in your planner which books you'll need to take home from that class. That way, you'll just have to take a quick look at your planner to know what you will need to bring home at the end of school.

Set Up a Homework Center

What does your study area look like at home? Is it on the kitchen table? Is it in front of the TV? Maybe it's in your room with the stereo turned up

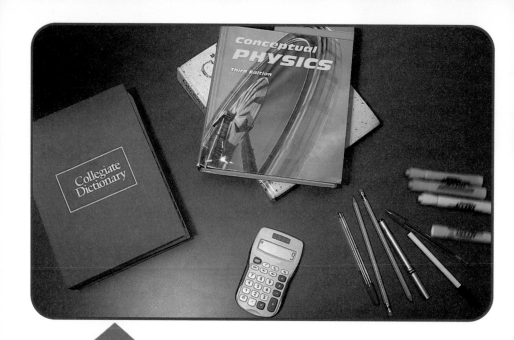

It's worth it to spend a minute or two laying all your supplies out before you start your homework. This way, you won't break up the flow of your studying later on.

loudly? If these are the environments in which you're working, you'll have trouble. Any place that provides too many distractions will make studying much harder. Everyone needs a place to work that cuts down on distractions. This place should be as quiet as possible. The space should also provide a place to store all your supplies. Keep your pens, pencils, calculator, highlighters, dictionary, and textbooks in one convenient spot. Setting up a good homework center at home will help you relax.

Dealing with Distractions

Finding a totally quiet work environment is not always possible. However, you can find ways to deal with distractions that do come up. First things first: Don't set up any distractions of your own! Turn off the TV, the radio, and the CD player. Also, shut down your computer (unless, of course, you're doing research).

Are your brothers or sisters the distraction? If so, try to find a quieter work place. If that's not possible, kindly ask them to keep it down. If all else fails, have a talk with the whole family. Try to set up a schedule that will give you quiet time during each evening.

Heads Up

CAUGHT IN THE WEB

The World Wide Web is an incredible study tool. It allows students to do quick research without leaving home. It provides instant paths to millions of amazing Web sites. Yet with all those choices, it's easy to get distracted from the main task—your homework. Make sure your online search doesn't lead you astray. If you're doing a report on colorful birds, don't follow a link to the Baltimore Orioles baseball team. Try to set a time limit for your Web searches. If you can't find the answer to your question quickly, ask a parent for help, or call a classmate.

Distractions don't always involve the outside world. Sometimes they come from inside your head! Imagine that you're doing your work, when all of a sudden, your mind starts to wander. You try to refocus on your homework, but you can't. What can you do? You may want to quickly write down what you're thinking about. It's a good way to get it out of your head. You can always come back to it later.

Your Personal Prime Time

Just because it's time to work doesn't mean you're ready to get down to business. Sometimes you have to do some mental gymnastics to get in the best possible studying shape.

We're at our best when we're alert and focused. When are you at your best—the morning, the evening, or right after school? Some people like to work right after school, while their minds are still in classroom mode. Others need to do something physical first, like taking a bike ride. Still others

Try to remain comfortable as you study—but not too comfortable! Distractions like loud music or the TV will keep you from completing your studies.

As long as this student uses his computer for research, it will be a powerful ally. If he starts playing video games, though, he'll get nowhere fast.

need to relax and collect their thoughts. Which type of worker are you? Try to schedule your studying for the time when you are most focused.

Sometimes you'll have to work even when you're not at your best. But you can make the most out of that time. If you have several things to do, choose a simpler task. Work on an assignment that doesn't involve reading long passages or taking notes. Take a few minutes to organize all your materials or clean your binders. Take a quick walk. Get some fresh air. Then get down to work!

SMARTER STUDIES

- Don't just read! Take notes, highlight passages, and jot down questions. Doing these things will keep you more focused.
- Set reasonable goals. Decide how much you want to accomplish in a certain amount of time, and try to stick to it. If you get the job done well ahead of schedule, try to do a little more next time.
- Plan to take breaks—and don't wait too long. Do something to energize yourself. Get your brain and your body moving.
- After a break, be sure to get right back to work. The longer you wait, the harder it will be to refocus.

When the teacher talks, you have to do more than listen—you have to write notes, too.

Chapter 3

Make a Note of It

As you get older, you're asked to take more notes while the teacher talks. This isn't easy. You have to listen, think, and write—all at the same time. However, good notes can really come in handy. They can condense an entire chapter into five minutes worth of reading. Here are ways to help you take better notes.

- Start each day's notes on a new sheet of paper. Write the date and subject on the top line.
- Try to write as many facts or ideas as you can.
- If the idea is particularly important, underline it, or put a star next to it.

By leaving her margins empty, this student can add a few extra remarks when she re-reads her notes.

- Mark the note with a question mark if you don't understand it. That way you can come back to it later, or ask the teacher to explain it after class.
- Don't write in full sentences! Doing so takes up too much time. Use short phrases.

- Use easily remembered abbreviations and symbols (see Heads Up box on page 26).
- Write neatly. Leave room between ideas in case you need to add something later.
- Leave the margins empty for later.
- Read over your notes as soon as you can. If something looks odd or incomplete, ask your teacher about it.

Taking Notes From a Book

Get a First Impression

Before you start an assigned reading, scan the headings, subheadings, and introduction. This will give you a clear first impression of the material.

Read in Chunks

Don't try to take notes on the whole thing at once. Read a small section. Once you're sure you understand it, take notes. Then move on to the next section.

Heads Up

The following abbreviations can be used while taking notes:

Abbreviation:	Means:
w/	with
w/o	without
& or +	and
b/c	because
ex	example
=	equals; is
≠	doesn't equal; is different from

Question and Repeat

As you read, questions usually go through your mind, even if you don't realize it. When you think of a question, write it on a Post-It™. Stick the Post-It™ next to the text. Think about what the teacher might want you to understand about that section. Don't forget to pay attention to any accompanying pictures, captions, and charts. There's often a lot of good information there. You'll remember the information better if you see a picture that is connected to it.

Try to paraphrase, or say in your own words, what you're reading. Don't copy the text word for word. You need to be able to say the ideas in your own words. Then you will truly understand and remember what you've read.

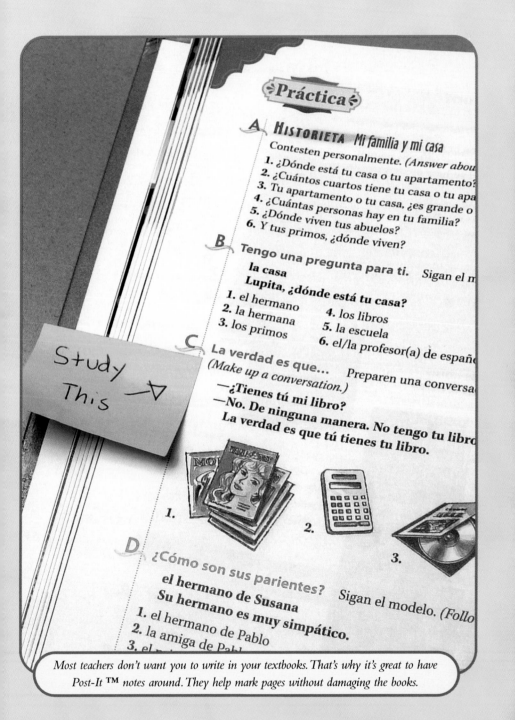

Práctica

A. HISTORIETA Mi familia y mi casa

Contesten personalmente. (Answer abou
1. ¿Dónde está tu casa o tu apartamento?
2. ¿Cuántos cuartos tiene tu casa o tu apa
3. Tu apartamento o tu casa, ¿es grande o
4. ¿Cuántas personas hay en tu familia?
5. ¿Dónde viven tus abuelos?
6. Y tus primos, ¿dónde viven?

B. Tengo una pregunta para ti.   Sigan el m

la casa

Lupita, ¿dónde está tu casa?

1. el hermano   4. los libros
2. la hermana   5. la escuela
3. los primos   6. el/la profesor(a) de españo

C. La verdad es que...   Preparen una conversa
(Make up a conversation.)

—¿Tienes tú mi libro?
—No. De ninguna manera. No tengo tu libro
La verdad es que tú tienes tu libro.

1.

2.

3.

D. ¿Cómo son sus parientes?   Sigan el modelo. (Follo

el hermano de Susana
Su hermano es muy simpático.

1. el hermano de Pablo
2. la amiga de Pabl
3. el

Most teachers don't want you to write in your textbooks. That's why it's great to have Post-It ™ notes around. They help mark pages without damaging the books.

27

Pete Gets Beat

Meet Put-it-off-Pete. Pete is a procrastinator. He puts off a lot of things, promising to do them later. He has a lot of work and responsibility, just like you. The difference is that he hasn't learned what you've learned about being school smart. Now he's gotten himself into a real jam.

It's 5:00 P.M. on Tuesday. Put-it-off-Pete has just come home from basketball practice. He has a big science test tomorrow, a book report due on Friday, and fifty math problems to do tonight. He meant to start studying for the test on Monday. Monday night would have been perfect, because his whole evening was free. Instead, he spent the evening watching a movie on TV. So, as usual, he now finds himself panicking.

In his room, Pete unpacks his books. He sits at his desk. He has all of his supplies in one drawer, so he's ready to go! He flips on his favorite CD and gets to work.

Well, not quite. First Pete listens to his favorite song a few times, to put him in the mood. Finally,

At the rate he is going, the only thing Put-it-off Pete will memorize is the song in his head.

he gathers the science notes that he took in class yesterday. He tries to pick out the important ideas. Unfortunately, he has written the notes in long, confusing paragraphs. He realizes that he doesn't fully understand the material. If only he had spoken with his teacher after class yesterday!

Pete sings along with his CD, tapping his pencil on the desk. Suddenly, he realizes that he's been reading the same pages over and over again. To make matters worse, he still doesn't know what he's reading. He can only remember the lyrics of his favorite song. He decides to switch to math, which he enjoys. He manages to get through most of his math problems by dinnertime.

After dinner, Pete gets back to work. Reading the science notes again, Pete starts thinking about the coming weekend. Could he get some guys together to play football? Will he go to the movies on Saturday? Maybe he should check online to see what movies are playing. This takes another 30 minutes, and he still hasn't done any work. The title of one movie, *Report for Duty*, catches Pete's eye. It makes him realize that he hasn't even started reading the book for his book report. He turns to the first page, but he's just too tired to read now.

Pete is also getting much more nervous about tomorrow's science test. He turns back to his science notes. He decides to read them over and over

By the time Pete starts getting serious on his homework, his best friends
have already finished the job.

until he at least memorizes some of the material.
Maybe tomorrow, he'll get to school early, hoping
his science teacher will be available for extra help.

Pete decides to call his friend Jess. Jess's mother
answers the phone. It seems that Jess is busy taking
a practice science test he got from the teacher.
Next, Pete calls his friend Tracy. Tracy's father tells
Pete that she has already gone to bed. Tracy wanted
to be well rested for tomorrow's test.

Why the long face, Pete? He's probably upset that he's going to have to get up at the crack of dawn. It's the only way he'll be able to cram in all the studying he should have done last night.

Pete sighs wearily. He's tired, nervous, and he knows he'll never accomplish any more work tonight. Pete decides to go to bed. He makes a pledge to set his alarm for 6:00 A.M. for some early morning cramming. Tomorrow is going to start roughly for Pete.

Let's take a closer look at poor Pete's situation. We'll examine what he did right and what he could have done differently.

Pete does have a homework area all set up, with supplies on hand. His first mistake, though, was putting on the CD while he worked. That little disc distracted him all night long.

Since Pete procrastinated the night before his test, he missed the opportunity to start studying Monday, when he had more time. He also should have found out when his teacher was providing extra guidance. Pete needs a calendar to remind him of upcoming tests and due dates.

Pete could also use some help in his note taking. His notes tended to ramble. If he'd just written down the main ideas, his notes would have been much clearer.

Pete gave himself breaks, but not for a specific period. Because of this, he wasted a lot of time. Once he finally returned to business, he found it hard to concentrate. It's not unusual for the mind to wander from time to time. When Pete's thoughts turned to the weekend, however, he should have just scribbled those thoughts down. Instead, he let them interrupt his studying.

Put-it-off-Pete learned a lesson from his frustrating night. Next time, he'll be more organized and focused.

Chapter 4

Testing, 1, 2, 3...

Let's face it: You're going to have tests, and you're going to have to study for them. There's no getting around it! However, you can help yourself successfully get through it.

Spread the Studying

Don't make the mistake of cramming right before a test. Study a little all week. Find out as soon as possible what material will be included on the test. Break that material down into smaller chunks. Study one or two chunks each night.

Rise to the Challenge

Try to hit the hardest stuff first. This will give you the whole week for the most difficult material to soak in.

It can be frustrating to try and solve your hardest homework at the end of the night. So rise to the challenge and tackle your tough assignments first.

Have someone give you a pre-test. This way, you can see what you already know, and what you need to work on more. Spend most of your time working on what you need to learn, not what you already know!

Write Your Own Test

This is a great way to study! If you know what type of test it will be (essay, true-false, multiple choice), write those types of questions. If you're not sure, write a few of each. Then have someone give you the test orally.

Test Day

Okay, you've completed all your studying. Now you're at your desk, about to receive the test. You may be a little nervous. Your heart may be beating too quickly, but fear not! You can be a champion test taker.

Overall Strategies

You have two main goals while taking the test. The first is to perform well. The second is to keep a

Heads Up

Here are some quick, easy ways to help you remember things:

- **Say it loud!** Reading material aloud is one of your memory's most powerful allies. You'll be absorbing the material through your eyes *and* ears!
- **That is to say....** If you paraphrase what you read, you'll be able to understand it better.
- **Use a trick.** Mnemonics is a fancy word that means using a short word or phrase to help you remember facts. Need to memorize the names of the Great Lakes? Think of the word HOMES: Huron, Ontario, Michigan, Erie, and Superior.
- **Repeat after me.** Memorizing facts can be a tough task. Repeating facts over and over will help strengthen your connection to them.
- **Each picture tells a story.** Try combining the information with mental images. For example, while studying single-celled animals, make a picture of one in your head. Can you see the little hairs on the side of the flagella?

This student wrote his own test the night before. Since he used the toughest questions he could find, the actual test seems like a breeze.

calm, positive attitude. Many times, if you take care of the second thing, the first will take care of itself.

• Write down what you know on a blank piece of paper the moment the test begins. You can refer to this page if there are many facts, such as formulas, dates, and names, you'll need to use. Be sure you get the teacher's approval before doing this.

- Take a minute to scan the entire test. Get an idea of what's coming. You might find a clue on the last page for a question on the first page!
- Don't beat yourself up because you can't answer one question. Simply move on to the next. Doing this will help you feel successful about the questions you do know. You can always come back to the tough question later.

Multiple-choice Questions

One of the main rules is to use the clues that these questions give you. Here are some tips.

- As they say on *Who Wants to Be A Millionaire*, use a 50/50. Cross-out all answers that you know are wrong.
- Underline key words in the question, such as *except*, *not*, or *always*. They'll give you important clues as to which answer to pick.
- Read through all the answers, even if you think the first one is definitely right. You may find another one that makes more sense.

Essay Questions

- Figure out exactly what the question is asking you to do. Rewrite it in your own words. If the question reads, "There are many metaphors in the second verse of the following poem," don't start looking for metaphors in the first verse. You'll waste your effort and time.
- Look carefully at the directions. Underline any key words. Is the essay question asking you to give a certain number of examples or details?
- Plot out what you plan to write before answering the question.
- Use an outline to sort out what you want to put in the essay, and where it would best fit (see example on page 46).
- Jot down details. Don't use complete sentences, just main ideas.
- Have it all planned out? Now use what you've done and write the essay!

To get a perfect score on an essay test, make sure you follow the directions to the letter.

New Words

budget to plan how many resources, especially time or money, will be spent at a certain time

concentrate to focus your mind in order to complete a task

expectations hopes of doing or getting something

guidance help or advice

mnemonics a system to develop or improve your memory

New Words

paraphrase to rewrite or restate, in your own words, something you've read or heard

peer a person who is, or is near, your own age

procrastinator someone who puts off doing things until a later time

schedule a plan of assignments or work to be completed by a certain time

strategies plans of action in order to meet a certain goal

For Further Reading

Fender, Gloria. *Learning to Learn: Strengthening Study Skills and Brain Power*. Nashville, TN: Incentive Publications, 1990.

Gilbert, Sara Dulaney. *How to Do Your Best on Tests*. New York: William Morrow & Co., 1999.

James, Elizabeth, Carol James, and Carol Barkin. *How to Be School Smart: Super Study Skills*. New York: William Morrow & Co., 1998.

Luckie, William R., and Wood Smethurst. *Study Power: Study Skills to Improve Your Learning and Your Grades*. Cambridge, MA: Brookline Books, 1997.

Schumm, Jeanne Shay, Ph.D. *School Power: Study Skill Strategies for Succeeding in School*. Minneapolis, MN: Free Spirit Publishing, 2001.

Resources

WEB SITES
RU Organized?
http://library.thinkquest.org/J002345/

Encarta – Homework Main
http://encarta.msn.com/homework/

Study Skills Topic Pages
www.how-to-study.com/

Ask Jeeves Kids' Reference Desk
www.ajkids.com/studytools/index.asp

Sample Essay Outline

Creating an outline before answering an essay test question is a key to success. Here's an example:

Essay: Explain three reasons why explorers came to the New World. What were they looking for?

Introduction	Explorers sent across world for different reasons In search of things they couldn't find at home
Reason 1: Gold	To bring back riches to king or queen No gold in Europe Found much in Mexico
Reason 2: Spices	Very few spices in Europe Were starting to eat foods from Far East Didn't have things like cinnamon, nutmeg, etc.
Reason 3: Spread religion	Wanted to convert natives to Christianity Natives could also be used as slaves
Conclusion	Many reasons explorers went— including gold, spices, religious Influenced countries they explored

Index

Index

About the Author

Nancy Golden started her career in children's publishing. She went on to work in children's animation, video, television, and licensing. For the past ten years, she has been an elementary school teacher, which she loves almost as much as she loves being a mother.